Let's visit
TUNISIA

MARY DIXON

ACKNOWLEDGEMENTS

The Author and Publishers are grateful to the following organizations and individuals for permission to reproduce copyright illustrations in this book:

C. M. Dixon; Hutchison Library Ltd; Ministry of Information, Tunis; Office National du Tourisme Tunisien, Tunis.

© Mary Dixon 1987

All rights reserved. No reproduction, copy or transmission of this publication may be made without written permission.

No paragraph of this publication may be reproduced, copied or transmitted save with written permission or in accordance with the provisions of the Copyright Act 1956 (as amended), or under the terms of any licence permitting limited copying issued by the Copyright Licensing Agency, 7 Ridgmount Street, London WC1E 7AE.

Any person who does any unauthorised act in relation to this publication may be liable to criminal prosecution and civil claims for damages.

First published 1987

Published by
MACMILLAN PUBLISHERS LTD
Houndmills, Basingstoke, Hampshire RG21 2XS
and London
Companies and representatives
throughout the world

Designed and produced by Burke Publishing Company Limited
Pegasus House, 116-120 Golden Lane,
London EC1Y 0TL, England.

Filmset in Baskerville by Datatrend, Hull, England.
Colour reproduction by Swift Graphics (UK) Ltd.,
Southampton, England.
Printed in Hong Kong

British Library Cataloguing in Publication Data
Dixon, Mary
Let's visit Tunisia.
1. Tunisia—Social life and customs—
Juvenile literature
I. Title
961'.105   DT252
ISBN 0-333-44990-8

LET'S VISIT TUNISIA

Contents

	Page
Map	6
Introducing Tunisia	7
The Land	13
Northern Tunisia, the Tell	15
Central Tunisia—the Steppes and the Sahel	19
The South	23
Ancient Civilizations	30
Islamic Rule	41
The French Protectorate and the Struggle for Independence	55
Tunisia Today—the Political System	62
Education and Welfare	66
Agriculture and Fishing	74
Industry, Tourism and Crafts	79
The Future	93
Index	94

TUNISIA

Map Labels

Cities and Towns:
- Bizerta
- Tabarka
- Menzel Bourguiba
- Ain Draham
- Béja
- Carthage
- TUNIS
- El Kef
- Dougga
- Nabeul
- Hammamet
- Kairouan
- Sousse
- Monastir
- El Jem
- Kasserine
- Sfax
- Gafsa
- Nefta
- Tozeur
- Kebili
- Gabès
- Douz
- Matmata
- Medenine
- El Borma

Geographic Features:
- Cap Bon
- KROUMIR MTS
- R. Medjerda
- HIGH TELL
- MEDITERRANEAN SEA
- Kerkenna Islands
- Chott el Jerid
- Island of Jerba
- GREAT EASTERN ERG
- SAHARA DESERT

Countries:
- ALGERIA
- LIBYA

Inset Map:
- SPAIN
- FRANCE
- ITALY
- GREECE
- TURKEY
- SICILY
- TUNISIA
- MOROCCO
- ALGERIA
- LIBYA
- EGYPT
- SAUDI ARABIA

Scale: 0–200 km / 0–100 miles

how very many children there are. About half the people in Tunisia now are under twenty years old. This makes it a hopeful and energetic country, but it also causes great problems—particularly in providing jobs for everyone.

As a newly developing country with limited natural resources, Tunisia is finding it difficult to keep pace with its growing population. At the moment, many Tunisian men go abroad to work, particularly to Saudi Arabia and Kuwait. The fact that Libya sent its Tunisian workers home in 1985 shows that this cannot be a permanent solution. Too many unemployed people still drift towards the cities, especially Tunis. As educational standards improve, Tunisians expect more from life. Tunisia therefore faces many challenges in the future.

Tunisian children. Tunisia has a very youthful population, with about half its people under twenty years of age

The Land

Tunisia forms part of the north-west tip of Africa that is bordered to the north by the Mediterranean Sea and to the south by the Sahara Desert. Because it is surrounded by sea and desert, the Arabs call it *Djerzira-al-Maghreb*—"the island of the west", a name that vividly describes its apparent separation from the rest of Africa. The word *Maghreb* (west) is used today as the name of this whole area, which includes the countries of Morocco, Algeria and Tunisia.

Tunisia is the smallest of the three countries, with an area of 164,150 square kilometres (63,400 square miles). It forms the eastern extremity of the Maghreb, so it is washed by the Mediterranean to the east as well as the north. In fact, it has over 1,300 kilometres (800 miles) of Mediterranean coast.

A great system of mountains unites the Maghreb. These mountains, known as the Atlas Mountains, run right across the region in parallel ridges from south-west to north-west. They actually form part of a series of Alpine mountain chains that surround the western Mediterranean. The range becomes lower and dies out in Tunisia, but reappears 140 kilometres (90 miles) away across the Mediterranean, in Sicily.

In most of the Maghreb the Atlas Mountains run parallel to the north coast, rising to form a barrier between the sea and the interior of the country. In Tunisia, however, they gradually die away to the plain of Tunis in the east. This has enabled two important ports, Bizerta and Tunis, to be developed there. Tunisia's gently shelving east coast has no mountains at all. It lies at right angles to the chains of the Atlas Mountains. This means that from earliest times outsiders have been able to enter Tunisia from the east and penetrate into the heart of the country.

The simplest way to describe Tunisia's physical variety is to divide the country into three main areas: first, the hilly north, including the High Tell Mountains and the Cap Bon peninsula; second, the open rolling steppe land in the centre that stretches to the east coast or Sahel; and third, the south of the country that lies beyond the final outcrop of the Atlas Mountains and merges into the Sahara.

The different regions of the country have different climates. The north has a Mediterranean climate, with warm summers and cool, sometimes wet, winters. Throughout the country rainfall is extremely variable from year to year. In the north the average annual rainfall ranges between about 40 and 60 centimetres (16 and 24 inches), while a few mountain districts receive as much as 100 centimetres (40 inches) in some years. Further south, in the Steppe and Sahel, the climate becomes hotter and drier. The rainfall is more erratic, and the annual rainfall is between 30 and 40 centimetres (12 and 16 inches). Further south still the climate becomes semi-arid, even arid in the desert of the far south, and rainfall is less than 20 centimetres (8 inches) each year.

NORTHERN TUNISIA, THE TELL

Two ridges of the Atlas Mountains stretch part of the way across northern Tunisia from the west. By the time they reach Tunisia the great limestone ridges of the Algerian Atlas have become the softer sandstones and clays of the Kroumir Mountains, which rise from the rocky north coast. They are not really high mountains, never rising above 1,500 metres (5,000 feet), but they remind the European visitor of the lower slopes of the Alps. They were popular as a holiday resort with the French colonizers earlier in the twentieth century, and the small, red-roofed houses on the wooded hillsides still have an air of French Alpine settlements. Now the area is popular in summer with Tunisians because it is refreshingly cool.

The slopes of the hills are quite densely wooded, and shelter a variety of wildlife. Hunters come to the Kroumirs to shoot

French-style red-roofed houses in the Kroumir Mountains

Cork oak trees in a forest in the Kroumir Mountains — the bark has been stripped away to be processed into cork

wild boar, which still roam here as they did in Roman times. Cork oaks are conspicuous in the forests because their trunks are a deep reddish-brown where the bark has been stripped away to be processed into cork.

The prevailing winds blow across the sea from the north-west and shed their rain on the northern hills. Unfortunately, these very hills then prevent the rain-bearing winds from penetrating further south, where rain is badly needed.

South of the Kroumir Mountains, there is a series of wider and higher ridges, known as the High Tell. The French called them the *Dorsale*, meaning "backbone". These hills are drier and less wooded, but the scenery is varied and often very beautiful.

Between the Kroumir range and the High Tell lies the valley of the Medjerda River. Although it rises in Algeria, the Medjerda and its system of tributaries form Tunisia's only really important and constantly-flowing river. It finds its way to the sea through the plain that lies between the Lake of Bizerta and the Gulf of Tunis. Much work is being done to improve irrigation in this area and consequently new villages are growing up along the valley.

The Medjerda valley is Tunisia's great cereal-growing area and has been in continuous cultivation for thousands of years. The fields are vast, as it has traditionally been an area of very large farms, and tractors can move in rows across the landscape. In the spring this wide valley is full of colour. But once the wheat and barley have been reaped the whole landscape looks brown

Harvesting wheat in the fertile Medjerda valley region

Picking tomatoes near Bizerta—many of Tunisia's vegetables are grown in this exceptionally fertile area

after the summer's heat. There are a number of small, but lively, towns in this area. Some of them, like El Kef, overlook the valley from the side of the hills. Many of them have existed for hundreds of years. The traditional wheat capital of this area is Béja.

Further east, nearer Bizerta, where the land is very fertile, agriculture is more diversified and many vegetables are grown. The most important of these are potatoes, tomatoes and the hot green peppers that the Tunisians love to use in their cooking. Tobacco is also grown here.

Just south of Bizerta, on the opposite side of the lake, is the town of Menzel Bourguiba, with its steel works and industrial complex. The north-eastern area is the most densely populated part of the country. At its fringe stands the capital, Tunis, with 800,000 people—eight times as many people as there are in the second largest town, Sfax.

South of the Gulf of Tunis, the Cap Bon peninsula stretches out to sea, as though reaching towards Sicily, to which some geographers think it may once have been joined. From Cap Bon, at the tip of the peninsula, Sicily can be seen on clear days. The peninsula is joined to the mainland by the fertile plain of Grombalia. Beyond the plain, on the peninsula, the Atlas Mountains revive again in a series of low hills, some of them given over to vine-growing. The east coast of the Cap Bon peninsula is being developed as a citrus-growing area. It has a particularly delightful mild Mediterranean climate and it is not surprising that its picturesque towns of Nabeul and Hammamet have become very popular with tourists.

CENTRAL TUNISIA—THE STEPPES AND THE SAHEL

Central Tunisia lies between the hills of the High Tell to the north and the desert to the south. It stretches over the steppes and the Sahel: the High Steppe inland, the Low Steppe to the east, and the Sahel along the coast. The High Steppe is a region of hills and wide, hollow valleys, which are sometimes cut through by large rivers, called *oueds* or wadis. These rivers dry up in the summer, but often flood for short periods in the winter. It is a dry region. The vegetation is mainly alfa (or esparto) grass, although there are some stunted forests.

Until the beginning of the twentieth century this was the land

Introducing Tunisia

Tunisia is not a large country, only about the size of England and Wales together, but it is a country full of contrasts. It lies at the eastern edge of the north-western tip of Africa, so it has the Mediterranean Sea to the north and east, and the Sahara Desert to the south. The landscape provides dramatic contrasts between cool wooded hills and hot wide plains, between noisy towns and lazy beaches, between arid desert and shady oases.

These contrasts in landscape are echoed by contrasts between the people of different regions. Businessmen in the cities look like businessmen everywhere, but in the country people keep to more traditional clothes. Many men wear a brimless round hat called a *chechia,* and many women wrap themselves in a large white shawl called a *safsari*. Bedouin women work in the fields and olive groves dressed in very colourful clothes, decorated with gold chains, discs and ear-rings.

The age-old contrast between settled agricultural workers and nomads who live in tents, moving with their animals in search of good grazing, is beginning to break down in Tunisia as more people are being encouraged to settle. Yet there is still a great difference between a prosperous farmer in the north, and the southerner with his goats or a few date palms to tend.

There are now nearly seven million people in Tunisia. During

A Bedouin girl in traditional costume

the course of several thousand years, the original inhabitants of Tunisia, the Berbers, have intermarried with the many other people who have invaded their land or been welcomed as settlers. These people have included Phoenicians, Romans, Arabs, Turks, Maltese, Jews, Italians and French. The descendants of all these people are now simply, and proudly, Tunisian. Perhaps it is their mixed past that has made the people so unusually friendly and tolerant—a Tunisian characteristic that all visitors notice.

Tunisia became an independent country in 1956. Its language is Arabic and its religion Islam. For some time before 1956, Tunisia had been ruled by France as a Protectorate, and this has left obvious marks on the country. The contrast between Arab and French cultures is most marked in the cities.

Some important cities, such as Tunis, the capital, and Sfax and Sousse on the east coast, are almost two cities in one. Each has at its centre the *medina,* the old Arab walled town. Here are the oldest mosques in the city, where men come individually to pray and to study the Quran, the holy book of Islam, and where they all meet for communal prayer on Fridays. Clustered round the mosques are the *souks*—winding streets of shops and work-rooms. Nearest the centre are the *souks* of the goldsmiths, jewellers and perfumers; further out are the shoemakers and leather workers; and at the edge are the butchers and food-

The *medina* — the old walled town of Tunis

A typical *souk* scene of shops and workrooms—in Tunis

sellers. These streets could exist anywhere in the Arab world.

Outside the *medina* lies the modern city. Tunis, Bizerta, Sfax and Sousse all have the boulevards, shops and pavement cafés that are familiar to any visitor to France. To these are being added modern offices and factories of international design. Although Arabic is the official language of the country, many people also speak French. Newspapers, advertisements and signs appear on the streets side by side in both languages.

Tunisia's geographical position and its history have given it a unique understanding of different points of view. Since independence Tunisia has always defended the right of other nations to have the governments of their choice, and has refused to interfere in the internal affairs of other countries.

It is eager to integrate itself with the other countries in north-west Africa, since this is where it belongs geographically and historically. To this end, it has steadily increased its co-operation with Morocco and Algeria, although its relationship with Libya presents greater problems.

As one of the most tolerant Islamic Arab countries, Tunisia has played an important part in trying to achieve a balance between the interests of different groups in the Middle East. As an African country, once ruled by a foreign power (France), Tunisia understands and supports the needs of developing states in the rest of the African continent. As a Mediterranean country, Tunisia looks towards the European Economic Community.

Tunisia's future will depend on its children. All visitors notice

An advertising hoarding in Tunis. Although Tunisia's official language is Arabic, French is widely spoken and the two languages often appear side by side and are understood equally well

where great rival tribes lived by breeding horses, sheep, goats and camels and by collecting alfa grass. This region is now being irrigated and improved where possible, and olive and almond trees and other seasonal crops have been introduced. As agriculture has improved, nomadic herdsmen have been encouraged to settle here. The town of Kasserine has been revived by the building of a factory making paper from wood pulp and esparto grass.

Further east, the Low Steppe stretches out monotonously over wide plains. There is nothing to create humidity or to act as a barrier to the drying winds: no sea, few trees, few houses. Hundreds of years ago it was possible to grow wheat on these

The Oued Sejnane—a typical *wadi* that dries up in the summer

A shepherd with his flock near Kairouan. For centuries, the land in this region has been used for grazing sheep and goats; as a result, the soil has eroded to sandy dust in many places

plains, but nomadic tribes have used it for centuries as grazing land for sheep and goats so that now the soil has eroded to sandy dust in many places.

From this plain rises Kairouan, one of the sacred cities of Islam. Eucalyptus trees have been planted around Kairouan. These in turn serve to give shelter to other trees—chiefly fruit and nut trees. Some parts of this area have also been developed for olive-farming, encouraging the growth of villages.

Although it is so dry, the steppe has good supplies of water lying underneath it. It is possible to bore down to this underground water and make use of it, and this gives some hope for the development of the area.

The Low Steppe, like the High Steppe, is crossed by watercourses that only flow after heavy rain. Rain in the autumn and winter usually comes in the form of stormy downpours, which actually make the watercourses overflow and create very damaging floods. Even if this does not happen, the watercourses here fan out and evaporate in small salt flats. To counteract these problems, a large barrage is now being constructed near Kairouan. This should both prevent flooding and conserve winter rain in reservoirs until it is needed.

The coastal area, or Sahel, which stretches from the Gulf of Hammamet to south of Sfax, has less rainfall than the north coast. Sousse, in the Sahel, actually has the same average yearly rainfall as Kairouan on the Low Steppe. The sea and its humidity soften the climate, however, and dry farming is possible all along this coast. In dry farming, any available water, such as dew, is carefully conserved and used.

The Sahel is dedicated to olive-growing, because olive trees can spread their roots wide to use any available moisture in the soil. Orderly rows of olive trees stretch as far as the eye can see, with the trees exactly spaced out in carefully cultivated soil.

The main towns along this east coast—Sousse, Monastir and, above all, Sfax—are commercial olive-oil centres, producing one of Tunisia's most important exports. These are all very busy and attractive towns. In fact, the intensively cultivated alluvial plain of the Sahel supports many villages and small towns. It

Picking olives in the Sahel region. Olive trees can grow in this area of low rainfall because they spread their roots wide to use any available moisture in the soil but little else will grow here

is a region of independent craftsmen and artisans as well as farmers. The population of the Sahel is next in size to that of the Tunis area.

THE SOUTH
The southern half of Tunisia is much drier than the north, and the land becomes more and more arid as the amount of rainfall decreases further and further south.

The southern tip of Tunisia is sandy desert—part of the Great

Camels in the Great Eastern Erg—an expanse of sandy desert stretching from Algeria into southern Tunisia

Eastern Erg which spreads from Algeria in the east. The only inhabitants are a few wandering desert nomads, soldiers guarding the frontiers with Libya and Algeria, and oil workers at the small oilfield at El Borma.

Just south of the town of Gafsa and west of Gabès are a series of huge depressions in the land, bounded by ridges of barren rocky hills. In the winter these depressions flood to form wide expanses of shallow water which have no outlet to the sea, but remain until they dry out in the spring and summer to leave smooth wide plains of dried mud sparkling with salt crystals. These depressions are known as *chotts*.

The largest of the depressions, called the Chott el Jerid, stretches about 80 kilometres (50 miles) from east to west and about 50 kilometres (30 miles) from north to south. A road crosses it from east to west, but it could not be used in the winter until a few years ago, when it was built up into a high causeway which now carries it above the winter floods.

Apart from the *chotts* and the sandy desert of the great Eastern Erg, most of the land is rocky desert or semi-desert growing a sparse vegetation which gives some food for small herds of sheep and goats. Where there are springs and where water can be drawn up from wells, small areas can be cultivated.

In a few places here and there in the desert, large springs of water rise, and a river or a stream runs a short distance before drying up and disappearing. These are the oases, and here the valleys formed by the springs are full of vegetation. Date palms grow thickly, carefully tended to give crops of dates of high quality for local use and for export to other parts of Tunisia and abroad. Under the canopy of date palms, the waters of the stream are diverted along hundreds of small channels to all parts of the oasis. The oasis is divided into small plots of land where fruit trees—oranges, peaches and apricots—as well as vegetables (and fodder for the animals) are grown, nourished by the water and shaded from the fierce heat by the palm trees, which actually like to have their heads in the sun.

Large oases like this are found at El Hamma, Douz, Kebili, Tozeur and Nefta, while at Gabès an extensive oasis runs right down to the sea coast.

Gabès is an important town in this southern region, with a large market and a port that is the terminal for the oil pipelines from El Borma. It is also a busy fishing port. Gafsa is an inland town to the north of the desert and the *chotts*. There, chemical industries make fertilizer and industrial chemicals such as phosphoric acid from the phosphates which are mined in the country to the west of Gafsa.

South of Gabès, along the coast, much of the land is rather barren, supporting only a few sheep and goats, but other areas are covered with regular plantations of olive trees.

The oasis of Nefta

A pit-dwelling at Matmata. Sheltered from the fierce heat of the sun, houses such as this are pleasantly cool

South of Gabès, but a little inland, are many interesting villages in the rocky, semi-desert landscape. At Matmata the inhabitants have made their houses by excavating a great hole in the solid rocky ground, tunnelling out from the hole to make underground passageways and rooms. Sheltered in this way from the hot summer sun, the houses are cooler and more pleasant than ordinary houses above the ground.

Another interesting form of local architecture is found near by, at Medenine and Tatouine and the small villages near them. These are the *ghorfas*, used as store-rooms for grain and olive oil. They are built with curved, vaulted roofs, side by side and on top of each other, facing inwards round the sides of a square. They were built like this for protection against raiders in the past, and many are still used for storage. Today, as protection is less necessary, some have been turned into shops to attract tourists, and one or two have been made into simple hotels for visitors.

The island of Jerba lies just off the coast, and traffic can drive onto the island along a modern road which follows an ancient causeway built by the Romans. The island is very hot in summer and mildly warm in winter. It has pleasant sandy beaches, and has become a popular holiday resort, with many large tourist hotels and its own small airport.

Away from the tourist areas, the island has many date palms and olive trees. In the villages, farmers, potters, weavers and

Ghorfas—these traditional, defensively-built storehouses at Medenine are now being used as shops displaying the craft of the weaver

A fishing port on the island of Jerba famous for its sandy beaches—the pots in the foreground are used to catch octopus

other craftsmen carry on a form of life that has changed little in hundreds of years, despite the effects of tourism.

Ancient Civilizations

In early times North-west Africa, the Maghreb, was influenced more by people from the Mediterranean and the nearer parts of Asia than it was by people from Africa south of the Sahara. There may have been a period in prehistoric times when grass grew in the Sahara and animals such as lions, elephants and giraffes roamed there. But by the end of prehistoric times severe climatic change had reduced the rainfall so that the area had become a dry desert, dividing North Africa from the rest of the continent. Oasis-dwellers and nomadic shepherds learned how to survive there, and traders crossed it from time to time; but for most people it formed a barrier. By the beginning of recorded history the people who had settled north of the Sahara were white-skinned.

The boundaries shown on the maps today did not exist then. The borders with Algeria on one side and Libya on the other were not drawn up until the sixteenth century. For most of its history Tunisia has been just one part of the Maghreb, but its position at the eastern end of the Maghreb has shaped its history in a particular way. The good harbours in the Gulf of Tunis and the great shallow gulfs of the east coast have made it inviting to a series of invaders, and its fertile coastal plains have encouraged the invaders to stay. Tunisia's history is the story of how a series of civilizations overlapped and merged with each other.

By the beginning of historical times, certainly by 1000 B.C., most of the Maghreb was populated by farmers living quite settled lives, growing wheat and barley and rearing animals. They had ploughs and they could work metal. In the drier regions many of them would move with their animals to better pastures according to the seasons, going to a second home for a time, and returning to their original homes as the seasons changed. Some of them may have been completely nomadic—constantly moving with their animals to find the best available grazing. Historians and archaeologists call these people Libyic. They lived in tribal groups headed by chieftains, and they were the descendants of neolithic (later stone age) farmers.

Very little is known about the Libyic people because they have left no written history of themselves. Archaeologists are beginning to discover more about them from the things they made, but they enter written history only when they are described by other people. From very early times the Greeks, who lived on the opposite shore of the Mediterranean, knew them and traded with them. The Greeks called them *Barbaroi,* their name for anyone they met who could not speak Greek. This name has stuck to them and today they are usually known to us by the English version of that name—Berber.

The Greeks were not the only traders in the Mediterranean. At the eastern end of the sea lived the Phoenicians. Their homeland was chiefly in what is now called Lebanon. It was a narrow strip of land, backed by mountains, with so few resources that the Phoenicians had to trade to survive. Their traders went out from their coastal cities, notably Tyre and Sidon, to trade in the south-western Mediterranean.

They rowed their small ships against the westerly winds, keeping close to the shore, and putting in to land each night. It was natural that they began making settlements along the North African coast to which they could return regularly.

Their first African settlements were probably at Utica, at the northern end of the Gulf of Tunis, and at Hadrumetum (now Sousse), on the east coast. By far the most important city they built there, however, was Carthage, which lies at the south of the Gulf of Tunis, near the modern city of Tunis.

There is a legend about the foundation of Carthage, which may contain some truth. It says that in 814 B.C. a Phoenician Queen called Elissa, and some of her nobles, were banished from their native land. After many adventures they landed in North Africa, where the inhabitants offered them a piece of land as large as they could enclose with an ox hide. Queen Elissa cunningly cut the hide into a very thin, long strip, like a piece of string, and so marked out enough ground to found her new home, Carthage, or *Qart Hashat*—"new capital city".

For a long time the city was no more than a base for Phoenician merchants. It was one of several colonies which the Phoenicians had established at the western end of the Mediterranean. In the sixth century B.C., however, their eastern homeland, Phoenicia, was conquered by the Babylonians, and

Carthage became the head of a new Phoenician empire in the west, called the Carthaginian Empire.

As the city grew, the Carthaginians took over a large area of fertile coastal land, extending eventually as far south as Sfax, in what is now north-eastern Tunisia. To support themselves they raised cattle, sheep and goats and grew cereals, vines, olives, figs and dates. They were good farmers and knew how to make use of dry lands, probably introducing to Africa new techniques of irrigation and terracing.

Traces of Carthaginian civilization can be seen today in Tunisia, in the foundations of cities, for example, and in sculptured gravestones, small carvings and metal objects. There are also examples of writing, based on the alphabet invented by the Phoenicians that is the origin of the Roman alphabet we use today.

The Carthaginian Empire flourished in North Africa until about 289 B.C. From that time the Carthaginians began to be troubled by resistance to their rule from some of the Berber population, many of whom must have been turned off their land by the Carthaginian settlers. However, a much greater threat was growing. The city of Rome was becoming more powerful, and its armies gradually moved south down the Italian peninsula to Sicily, where they met and fought with the Carthaginians. This was the beginning of three long and bitter wars between Rome and Carthage, which are known as the Punic Wars. (The word "Punic" comes from the Roman name, *Poeni,* for the western Phoenicians, or Carthaginians.)

A Punic moument to the dead at Dougga

Rome crushed Carthage completely in 146 B.C. and the Romans are said to have burnt the city of Carthage to the ground. There are also stories that they then ploughed salt into the land so that nothing would grow there again. It is more likely that the salt was ritually sprinkled somewhere there to represent Rome's destruction of the city it hated.

The Romans' aim was simply to prevent Carthage ever becoming powerful again, so they took over the Carthaginian area of what is now north-east Tunisia. They called this area

Africa, and ensured that its people paid them tribute, but they did not extend their territories in *Africa* and make them fully part of the Roman Empire until about one hundred years later. By 25 B.C. they had united Tunisia and nearby Tripolitania (part of present-day Libya) into one large province called *Africa Proconsularis*; and they had taken over eastern Algeria, which they called *Numidia.*

The Roman army then set to work to Romanize *Africa Proconsularis* with typical thoroughness. They rebuilt Carthage as a Roman town. They built roads, and they divided land for cultivation into regular plots—the outlines of these can still be seen in places. Most amazing of all, they created a southern boundary to their African territory, to discourage raids by the desert nomads. This boundary was called the *limes*. It followed the natural boundary between the steppe and the desert, using stretches of ditch and wall to link natural barriers such as the *chotts* and the mountains. Having done that, they set about irrigating this southern land so that they could cultivate it. In fact, they cultivated land further south than anyone has ever done until now, when the Tunisians are beginning to bring that land back into use, with modern methods of irrigation. The remains of wells, dams and aqueducts throughout the country show how skilful the Romans were in finding, storing and transporting water.

All this was not done to feed the Romans in *Africa*. Wheat and barley were needed to feed the growing population in Rome itself. The most fertile parts of Tunisia became a vast granary

The remains of a Roman aqueduct near Tunis

for Rome. Such was the demand for wheat and barley that the growing of traditional crops, such as vines and olives, was actually forbidden in *Africa* during the first period of Roman occupation.

Strong Roman rule of the area brought many changes. Rich men in Rome bought large estates in *Africa*, which were farmed by tenant farmers, or *coloni*, and by slaves. As the province prospered, the population increased and many new towns were built. Some of these were on the sites of existing Punic towns; Roman mosaic floors laid on top of Punic floors can still be seen today.

The new towns had typically prestigious Roman public buildings—capitols and temples, triumphal arches, theatres and large public baths—as well as the necessary houses, workshops, aqueducts, roads and drains. It is possible to walk today in the ruins of towns such as Dougga, Thuburbo Majus, Bulla Regia, Maktar and Sufetula, and to imagine the rush of life through the narrow streets, the hubbub of the bathhouse and the grandeur and beauty of the colonnaded temples. Details conjure up the richness of the period—the olive presses at Sufetula, the cool underground houses of Bulla Regia and the pictures of contemporary life on mosaic floors everywhere. At El Jem the huge Roman colosseum squats on the plain, a reminder of the brutality of Roman life. Here, for the entertainment of thousands of spectators, men fought with each other, or with wild animals, to the death.

To supply food for these towns, mixed farming was again

A street in the remains of the Roman city of Dougga

A Roman mosaic excavated in Tunisia, dating from around the fourth century A.D., depicting life on a prosperous country estate

officially allowed. Because the Romans had superb techniques for conserving moisture in the soil, they were able to plant olive trees in the dry lands of the Sahel—as the Tunisians still do. Oil from these olives was used throughout the Roman Empire for preparing food, as fuel for lamps, and to clean and soothe the skin.

It was possible for peasants from the original population to prosper and advance through gaining Roman citizenship, but the majority of African people remained as serfs (who could be sold with their land to a new landlord), or as landless labourers paid only at harvest time, or simply as slaves. Many of the native population were pushed south to uncultivatable land, and must have become nomads.

During the Roman occupation, the new religion of Christianity spread fast in Africa. For a long time, the Romans distrusted Christians and persecuted them cruelly—for example by presenting them as part of the spectacle at El Jem, where they were sent into the walled arena and thrust towards ravenous beasts for the "entertainment" of the audience.

Life improved for Christians early in the fourth century, when the Roman Emperor Constantine accepted Christianity as the official religion of Rome. At this time too, Constantine moved the capital of the Roman Empire away from Rome itself, which was threatened with invasion. A new Christian capital was

The Colosseum at El Jem, where Christians were sent into the arena to be killed by wild animals, watched by a huge audience

established at Byzantium (now Istanbul) at the eastern end of the Mediterranean. From this period the empire is known as the Byzantine Empire, and colonies such as Carthage were ruled from there.

The Byzantine rulers were, however, driven out of Carthage in A.D. 439 by the Vandals. These were tribes from northern Europe who had been steadily advancing through Europe. The Vandals drove out the Byzantine rulers and remained in northern Tunisia for almost a hundred years. They did not leave any buildings or new systems of agriculture behind them, however, as other invaders have done. They never tried to extend their rule far inland, so it was an unsettled time, and it gave the Berbers the opportunity to become increasingly independent again.

In the year 533, the Byzantines defeated the Vandals and returned to rule Tunisia. Their rule was under constant attack from the Berber inhabitants, however, and in 646 the province was declared independent of Byzantium. Many of the Byzantine monuments remaining from that period are ruined fortresses.

Islamic Rule

In the seventh century came new invaders, from a new direction, bringing a new religion. It was the beginning of the most profound influence of all in Tunisia—that of the Arabs. To understand the effects of this invasion it is necessary to understand something of the beginning of the Muslim faith.

In about A.D. 610 in Mecca, a town in Saudi Arabia, a man called Muhammad claimed that the Archangel Gabriel had told him that he was to be the special Prophet through whom the will of God would be revealed to all men. The message from God that Muhammad gave to the people of his time was "There is no God but God. Muhammad is the messenger of God."

The Arabs to whom Muhammad had brought this message had always lived in tribes, and the tribes often fought each other. They believed in a supreme God, *Allah*, but in fact each tribe worshipped its own god. Muhammad now taught them that all men should submit themselves to the will of the one true God. This submission is called *Islam* and the true believer who submits himself in this way is a *Muslim*. A true Muslim will not only profess his faith but also perform four major duties. First, he must pray to God at five set times each day, no matter where he is or how inconvenient it might be. Second, he must give alms to the poor. Third, he must fast at set times. Fourth, he must, if possible, at least once in his lifetime, make a pilgrimage to Mecca, the place where the will of God was revealed to Muhammad.

In 622 Muhamad and his followers moved to the town of Medina, also in Saudi Arabia. Muslims use this date as the beginning of their era, just as Christians use the date of the birth of Christ as the first year in their calendar. From this time the movement based on Muhammad's teachings gained in strength.

Once the warring Arabian tribes began to submit to this single faith, to become Muslims, they also in a sense became equals, brothers in one faith. Men prayed on their own five times each day, and congregated for prayers, led by an *imam*, on Fridays at midday. The new faith united them and there was no longer any point in tribes fighting each other. Instead, they combined their energies and made probably the most remarkable series of conquests the world has ever known. Muhammad died in 632. By 750 the Arabs had created an Islamic empire that stretched from Spain and the Maghreb in the west to the River Indus (in Pakistan) in the east.

Unlike earlier invaders, the Arabs attacked what is now Tunisia by land, but they did not find it easy. Starting from Arabia, they had rapidly taken Egypt and Tripolitania, but then they had to move north through a region of desert that stretched down to the coast and therefore exposed them to attack from the sea by Byzantine ships. In 647 they made their first brief raid into Tunisia for booty. On their third expedition, in 670, they took a firmer hold on the old Roman colony of *Africa*, which they called *Ifriqiyah*, from which Tunisia has developed.

Their leader, Uqba ibn Nafi, established a city called Qayrawan (Kairouan) in the central steppe-land of Tunisia, away from the people he knew would be troublesome. These were the Byzantines on the coast, the Berbers in Numidia (present-day Algeria) to the west, and the group of Berber tribes called the Zenata who lived on the fringes of the Sahara in the south. In time, the Arabs built up a fleet, and in 698 they took Carthage from the Byzantines. Then they enlarged the port of

A mosque in the town of El Kef. Less than one hundred years after the death of Muhammad, the religion he preached had spread as far west as Spain and the Maghreb and as far east as present-day Pakistan

Tunis that lay in the sheltered waters of the lagoon at the end of the Gulf of Tunis. It became their second city after Kairouan, and eventually gave its name to Tunisia.

From their base at Kairouan the Arabs sent out expeditions that defeated the Numidian Berbers and the Zenata tribes, who had been fighting under the leadership of a woman called Kahina—"the priestess". By 711, North-west Africa was under the control of the Arabs. They recruited Berbers into their army and then moved on across the Straits of Gibraltar into Spain. Eventually they created the new Province of Spain and North-west Africa for the Arab Empire. This province was governed from Kairouan.

The Arabs brought with them their religion of Islam. Christianity was quite widespread in North-west Africa when they arrived, particularly in the coastal area, but it was confusing in its variety of beliefs. It had, however, spread a belief in one God, which Islam shared, and had thus paved the way for the new religion. In many ways the Muslim code, with its insistence on individual prayer and responsibility, was more suited to the tribal way of life of the Berbers than Christianity had been. There were also two practical reasons for people to become Muslims: Berbers who joined the Muslim army and became Muslims took a share of any booty they captured, and Muslim landowners paid no taxes.

Islam had its divisions and disagreements, just as Christianity had. The divisions arose shortly after the death of Muhammad and were caused chiefly by arguments about who should succeed him, as the interpreter of his words, his traditions and his laws. This disagreement continues today.

Some felt that Muhammad's successor should be chosen from among those men who had been his companions while he was formulating Islam; others felt that the successor should be a direct male descendant of Muhammad. As Muhammad left only a daughter (Fatimah), her husband, Ali (who was also Muhammad's cousin), was their choice. The division was broadly between the Sunni, or orthodox, Muslims and the Shi'ites who believed, among other things, that their leader should be a descendant of Ali and Fatimah. The first caliphs (rulers) of the Arab Empire ruled from Damascus and were from the orthodox group, but in 750 the Abbasids, who were Shi'ites, began to rule the Arab Empire from their new capital in Baghdad.

The western Arabs of North Africa felt very remote from the rulers in Baghdad: and, in 800, a western Arab, Ibrahim ibn al Aghlab, was appointed governor of Ifriqiyah. This was the beginning of a great period in Tunisian history. From 800 to 909 he and his successors, known as the Aghlabids, ruled there almost as independent sovereigns. They dominated not only Tunisia but the whole central Mediterranean area.

Under the Aghlabids, Kairouan became an outstandingly beautiful city, an intellectual centre and, spiritually, one of the four chief cities of Islam. The Great Mosque, originally built when the Arabs first settled in Kairouan, was rebuilt to twice its former size. Today, it still dominates the city when seen from

The prayer room of the Great Mosque of Kairouan

a distance across the plain. Its vast, sun-filled courtyard contrasts with its shady, tranquil prayer room. The ceiling of the prayer room is supported by a forest of slender columns. Many other beautiful and intricately decorated mosques were built in Kairouan; similarly, the great Zitouna mosque was built in Tunis, and there were others in Sousse and Sfax. The Aghlabids also built themselves palaces outside Kairouan, and they devised cunning systems of waterworks to conserve the winter rains. Some of their reservoirs still remain near Kairouan to this day.

Early in their settlement of Ifriqiyah, the Arabs built a number of fortified buildings (called *ribats*) along the coast as a defence against invasion by Byzantine Christians. The *ribats* were fortified monasteries in which pious Muslim warrior-monks lived. These buildings provided defence, centres for Muslim learning, and hospitality for pilgrims on their way to Mecca. The strong, severe outlines of the *ribats* often present an interesting contrast to the graceful curves of a nearby mosque of traditional design.

In 909 the Aghlabid civilization in Ifriqiyah was overthrown by Shi'ite Muslims whose rulers, the Fatimids, moved their capital from Kairouan to Mahdia on the east coast of Tunisia. Their rule was harsh and led to numerous revolts, which they successfully repressed. In 973 they felt sufficiently confident of their power to invade Egypt and set up rule there in their new capital, Cairo. They left Ifriqiyah under the rule of a Berber governor called Ziri, and his successors, the Zirids.

The *ribat* at Monastir. Founded originally in A.D. 796 to be both a fortress and a monastery, it has been repeatedly extended and restored

Ifriqiyah prospered under the Zirids, who restored some of its former culture and wealth. They made the mistake, however, of trying to break their ties with their Fatimid rulers in Cairo. These rulers decided to punish Ifriqiyah, and they found a very effective way of doing it.

Two very troublesome Bedouin tribes, the Banu Hilal and the Banu Sulaym, had recently spread to Egypt from the deserts of Arabia. The rulers in Cairo unleashed these tribes on Ifriqiyah and encouraged them to take whatever they wanted.

A later Arab historian, Ibn Khaldun, says that they "swarmed across the land like locusts", destroying everything as they went. He says elsewhere, of Arab tribesmen in general:

> *Arabs need stones to set them up as supports for their cooking pots, so they take them from buildings which they tear down to get the stones. . . Wood too is needed by them. . . for use as tent poles. So, they tear down roofs to get wood.*

This is obviously the reaction of a city-dweller to nomadic invaders, but even allowing for exaggeration, it seems likely that over a period of time 200,000 tribesman flooded into Ifriqiyah and changed everything.

In the areas where they penetrated the old Berber tribes disappeared, merging with the invaders. The invading Arabs were unlike the settled Arab town-dwellers already in Ifriqiyah. They spoke a different, non-classical Arabic language, which spread among the country people, and to which the rural Tunisian Arabic dialect of today is related. It was, in fact, the tribesmen rather than the great Arab educators who played the major part in making the population of Tunisia Arabic-speaking.

At the same time as the nomadic tribes were spreading through Ifriqiyah, Christian armies were trying to reassert themselves against the Muslims. The Christian Normans conquered Sicily, and then took Jerba in Ifriqiyah in 1134. They were soon expelled, however. From the turmoil there emerged a new dynasty of rulers of Ifriqiyah. These were the Hafsids, who were Berber in origin.

The Hafsids maintained their rule for the next three centuries (from 1230 to 1574). Under this new, tolerant Muslim rule, Tunisia re-established its importance in Mediterranean trade. Partly because it was once again looking to the Mediterranean, the port of Tunis now became the capital city instead of Kairouan. In addition, European merchants came to live in Tunis and it became an important commercial centre.

Another group of Muslims, with different cultural traditions, now settled in Tunisia. They were the Muslims from Spain who came to Tunisia after they had been driven out by the Christians who had reconquered Spain. These Andalusians brought with them their own distinctive, delicate forms of architecture and decoration, which have become an important part of Tunisian tradition.

The boundaries of Tunisia were still not settled. At the peak of their power the Hafsids governed not only the area now called Tunisia but also Tripolitania and part of Algeria. Boundaries still had no meaning, because in the interior of the country it was tribes of people rather than areas of land that had to be governed, and tribes of people moved about. All through this period intermarriage between Arabs and Berbers continued to blur the distinctions between them.

Under the Hafsids, Tunisia became the most stable and prosperous of the kingdoms of North Africa, but the Hafsids did not develop a strong army, and the smoothness of life could not survive the violent events of the sixteenth century. At that time Christians, Muslims and independent privateers struggled for power in the lands surrounding the Mediterranean. Tunisia suffered from being in the middle of these struggles.

From the confusion, a new power emerged. Gradually, the Turks from the eastern end of the Mediterranean came to

A traditional inner courtyard on show in the Arab section of the Bardo Museum in Tunis

dominate the area. As Muslims they were not unwelcome in North Africa. They established the new Islamic empire of the Ottoman Turks in the Mediterranean region.

Tunisia came under Turkish rule in 1574, and thus became a Regency of the Ottoman Empire, whose capital was in Constantinople (Istanbul), the former Byzantine capital. Tripolitania and Algeria also became Regencies and the boundaries between Libya, Tunisia and Algeria were drawn up and at last became much as they are today.

For the next two hundred years Tunis, in common with other ports of the North African coast, became not only famous for its traders but greatly feared for its privateers. These were not simply pirates, but sailors who were licensed to attack foreign, particularly Christian, ships and then to trade their prisoners for agreed ransoms, or to sell them as slaves.

Yet, in spite of its fearsome reputation, Tunisia impressed European travellers who braved the interior by the politeness of its inhabitants, the wealth of its agriculture and the charms of its scenery. Its society was well-ordered, but underdeveloped; the economy was based still on commerce and traditional agriculture and crafts. The country exported wool, leather, grain, dates and olive oil.

Tunisia maintained a certain independence from the Ottoman Turkish Empire, although it continued to receive pashas, or rulers, from Constantinople until the beginning of the eighteenth century. In 1705, a military leader took power. He was called Husain ibn Ali, and the dynasty he founded in 1710 was therefore called the Husainid dynasty. It survived until 1957. The dynasty in some ways restored Tunisia to its situation under the Hafsids. By the standards of the time, Tunisia had a stable rule that was accepted both by its own subjects and by the major Mediterranean powers.

The standard of government varied, however, with the talents of each individual ruler. On the whole, little was done to develop the resources of the country, to organize an army, to build roads or, most important, to improve the living conditions of the people.

In the nineteenth century Europe once again played a part in the affairs of Tunisia. By this time the European nations had become industrialized, richer and more competitive with one another. They were looking for opportunities to invest their new wealth and to expand their power.

The ruler of Tunisia from 1837 to 1855, Ahmed Bey, was very impressed by the luxury of European life and determined to attempt some schemes of modernization in Tunisia. To do this he began to borrow money at a high rate of interest from European banks, particularly French ones. Unfortunately, he also spent a great deal of money on personal extravagances, such as a new palace.

By 1869 Tunisia owed much more money to European banks than it could ever repay. The country was bankrupt. An International Commission was put in charge of its finances.

Tunisia had always hospitably encouraged representatives of the European countries with whom she traded to live in Tunis. During the first half of the nineteenth century, the representatives of England, France and Italy constantly competed with one another to gain influence and power in Tunisia, for example by building railways, tramways and a telegraph system.

France had already occupied Algeria by force in 1830 and was now looking for an excuse to enter Tunisia. In the spring of 1881, there was trouble with some tribes in the Kroumir Mountains whose land straddled the border between Algeria and Tunisia. This served as an excuse. On the pretext of putting down the trouble, French troops crossed from Algeria into Tunisia, and were not resisted.

In May 1881, an agreement was signed giving France the right to occupy Tunisia with her soldiers and to control Tunisia's foreign affairs. In June 1883, the Treaty of La Marsa established the French Protectorate of Tunisia.

The French Protectorate and the Struggle for Independence

The Protectorate was, in theory, different from conquest. It gave France the right to have its troops in the country. It also meant that the Bey, or ruler, of Tunis had to promise to undertake any reforms, other than religious ones, that the French thought necessary. In return, France guaranteed a large loan of money to the Bey.

Gradually, the French used their position to introduce reforms, some of which were necessary and useful. What they saw as reforms, however, the Tunisians often felt to be unwelcome interference in their way of life, and sometimes actual deprivation. These "reforms" led increasingly to France treating Tunisia as a colony, ruled directly from France, rather than as a protectorate.

In other words, France began to use Tunisia for its own profit and advantage and to run the country in a way that suited the French rather than the Tunisians. This shows most clearly in changes the French made in four areas: the structure of government, land ownership, the running of the economy, and education.

The French actually governed Tunisia through their Resident-General, although the Bey was still sovereign in name. There was also a Tunisian prime minister, and a council of ministers that included both Frenchmen and Tunisians. There was soon a very large French civil service. The only area of administration that remained open to Tunisians was at local level, which often involved the unpopular task of tax collecting.

One of the first changes made by the French was in the system of land ownership. The Islamic system in Tunisia was extremely complex. From 1885, the French passed a series of acts and decrees that attempted to simplify the situation and make it possible for individuals to buy land in the European manner. Previously some of the land had been under the control of the Bey, some held in trust for religious foundations and some owned collectively by nomadic tribes.

Now, good agricultural land became available. Some of this was bought by the wealthier Tunisian farmers. Much of it, however, was bought by large French companies. Prices put it far above the reach of poor Tunisians. Yet in the past many of them had had traditional rights to farm and some of them had been able to use the land held in trust. Now they were turned off the land they had thought of as theirs. By 1897 the French owned one-sixth of all the useful agricultural land in the country, although there were very few French settlers.

Their system of agriculture was quite different from that of the Tunisians. They farmed larger units in a more efficient way with fewer workers. They produced crops for other people to buy—"cash crops". The small Tunisian farmers had farmed not to sell their crops but to obtain food for themselves and their family. This is called "subsistence farming". It is not efficient in financial terms, but it provides employment and a sparse living for more people. It was also more flexible since in hard times nomadic tribes could move from the arid lands to lands in better areas. Now that was no longer possible.

The change in land ownership affected the economy of the country. Farmers who had lost their land, and those who could no longer find work on the more "efficient" farms, migrated to the towns where they lived in misery in squalid, makeshift huts.

During this period, at the end of the nineteenth and the beginning of the twentieth century, the number of people in Tunisia increased, making the problem even worse. There was not sufficient industry in the towns to offer alternative employment. In fact, cheap, machine-made goods from France began to flood the market so that for a time even the craftsmen and artisans of Tunisia had no work.

There was some new employment, on newly constructed tramways in Tunis, for example, but these jobs went to the many Italians who had come to live in Tunisia. Wherever Tunisians could find work they earned much less than either French or Italian workers. The early twentieth century was a time of economic despair in Tunisia, which simply became worse at the time of the world-wide depression in the 1930s.

It was hoped that the French would develop education in Tunisia, particularly scientific studies. They did introduce primary schools, but these were on the French model; and by 1892 only twelve per cent of school places were occupied by

The Zitouna mosque in Tunis founded in A.D. 732

Tunisians compared with eighty-four per cent by French children. Muslim education continued at the Zitouna Mosque and University. The French did encourage the growth of Sadiki College, already in existence, where Arabic and French studies continued side by side. Later they established other similar secondary schools, notably the Lycée Carnot. Very able Tunisians were able to progress from these schools to university in France.

If the French hoped to turn educated Tunisians into loyal Frenchmen they were mistaken. It was from the Sadiki College that a group of men emerged who were to demand, and finally obtain, independence for Tunisia.

To begin with, some Tunisians had welcomed the Protectorate as an opportunity to co-operate with the French in modernizing Tunisia and destroying the power of the Bey. Gradually they came to resent the way France seemed to want them to become French. The French presence actually increased the Tunisians' belief that Tunisia was a nation with its own history and tradition.

This belief was expressed in 1920 by the foundation of a political party called the Destour Party. *Destour* is Arabic for "constitution", and the party said that because Tunisia had been given a constitution in 1861 it was already a nation and should not be assimilated by France. The party was run largely by members of the traditional ruling class in Tunis, but gradually ordinary workers too began to make their views felt. In 1934, some members of the Destour Party, who believed that Tunisia should become completely independent from France, broke away and founded a new party, called the Néo-Destour or New Constitution Party.

The foremost member of this party was Habib Bourguiba, who was later to become President of his country. Like other leading members of the party, he had been educated at Sadiki College and then in France. He had absorbed French culture, but he also believed that the strength of Tunisian society lay in its Islamic culture. He thought that Tunisia should move towards independence step by step, taking any opportunity that presented itself, and that Tunisians from all levels of society should join together in this effort. In 1942, during the Second World War, troops of the Allied Powers (England, America and France) invaded North Africa in an attempt to drive out the armies of fascist Germany and Italy. Bourguiba told the Tunisians they must support the Allied Powers, even though it meant supporting the French. This was because he feared colonization by fascist Italy.

After the war, in 1945, the Tunisian people submitted a manifesto to the United Nations Organization, asking for complete independence, and were bitterly disappointed when they did not get it. The French imprisoned Bourguiba for long spells, but when he was free he travelled the world seeking support for Tunisia's cause. He was strongly supported at home, not only by his party but by the UGGT—the Union of Tunisian Workers.

After 1952 there were long talks between Tunisia and France when France made half-promises and then broke them. At last, in June 1955, the French signed a convention that recognized the Tunisian right to self-government. When Bourguiba returned to Tunis from this successful meeting in France, an estimated 400,000 Tunisians turned out to give him a hero's welcome.

In March 1956 Tunisia became completely independent, in charge of its own affairs. Its first Constituent Assembly met in

Habib Bourguiba being given a tumultuous welcome on his return from France in June 1955, having secured Tunisian independence

April of that year, and Habib Bourguiba presided. Some people wanted a constitutional monarchy and a multi-party state. The majority of people, who had seen the strife in other newly independent states, wanted one party and one leader. So the Néo-Destour Party and Habib Bourguiba came to power.

Tunisia Today—the Political System

One of Tunisia's first acts after becoming independent was to hold elections for a Constituent Assembly. The Néo-Destour Party was overwhelmingly elected to power. Their task was to draft a constitution for their country, an expression of the beliefs and rules on which its government should be based. Knowing how important it was to get this right, they spent three years on the task.

At the begining of these three years Habib Bourguiba became President of the Council—Prime Minister, in other words. Very soon afterwards, in July 1957, the Assembly proclaimed Tunisia a republic. Bourguiba then gave up the office of President of the Council and was elected instead President of the Republic.

The constitution was introduced in 1959. From that time Tunisia has officially had presidential government. This means it puts the power to make decisions entirely in the hands of the president. According to the constitution, the president should be elected every five years. Because of President Bourguiba's heroic efforts to gain Tunisia's freedom, and consequently his special place in the people's affection, he was made president for life in 1974. If a president should die in office the constitution says that the prime minister will assume his authority until new elections take place.

A statue of President Bourguiba, who was made president for life in 1974

The Tunisian one-party system, from which the president is elected, has been different from such a system in any other country. Many Tunisians prefer to call it a "mass-party" system, to suggest the breadth of its support. The Néo-Destour Party existed a long time before independence, and was founded chiefly to secure that independence. It therefore includes people of very different political views who are bound together chiefly by their desire for the well-being of their nation. It has been called the Socialist Destour Party, or PSD (Partie Socialiste Destour) since 1964, and is concerned that every person should have equal opportunities.

Tunisia has been fortunate in its first president, Habib Bourguiba, who clearly enjoys being given such titles as "father of the nation" and "supreme combatant". He regarded the struggle for independence as only the first step in a continual struggle to improve conditions for the Tunisian people. He has not imposed a set of ideas on his people, but has tried to be flexible and move step by step towards overcoming Tunisia's huge social and economic problems that include poverty, illiteracy and unemployment. The fact that he was educated in both Tunisia and France has given him a mixed Islamic and European cultural background and a broad-minded approach to problems.

There has inevitably been opposition to his rule. On the whole he has managed to put down opposition without being vindictive, and to bring his opponents back into government later. Much of the opposition has come from the trade unions who wanted political and union life to be reorganized on a multi-party basis. In 1978 members of the main union, the UGGT, demonstrated in support of their views and were harshly treated.

After 1980 when a new prime minister, Mr. Mzali, was appointed there seemed to be a movement towards greater political freedom. President Bourguiba said he saw nothing against the emergence of other political parties as long as they rejected violence and religious fanaticism and were not dependent upon any foreign group.

In 1983 the President decreed that two main opposition parties should be given legal status. These were the Democratic Socialist

Movement (MDS) and the United Popular Movement (MUP). These parties then called for the legalization of other opposition parties. Yet throughout the second half of 1983 the government took strong action against the Popular Revolutionary Movement (MPR) and the Islamic Tendency Movement (MTI).

One of the main tests of Bourguiba's strength was the "bread riots" of January, 1984. Late in 1983 the government subsidy on flour and other cereals was removed; over night the price of bread more than doubled. To poor people, used to cheap bread as a main item of food, this was disastrous. Serious riots spread through many cities. The subsidy was resumed and order restored. Many of the people who were tried for their part in these riots were later pardoned or given light sentences, and blame for the situation was heaped on to the Minister of the Interior at the time.

The President originally showed what his priorities were by the sweeping reforms he made between 1956 and 1959—that is, in the three years between the achievement of independence and the introduction of the constitution. The changes he made then in education, the position of women, the ownership of land and the reorganization of justice are still being felt today.

Education and Welfare

At the time of independence only a small proportion of Tunisians were receiving any education. President Bourguiba saw education as one of the chief priorities of the new nation. He wanted to unify the system, to expand it drastically and to make it appropriate to the needs of Tunisian people. In 1958, he introduced reforms that could not begin to show results until the 1970s.

First, he brought the great Islamic University, the Zitouna, into the State system by making it the theological faculty of the University of Tunis. He also reduced religious education in the primary schools to one or two hours a week. In this way, education was taken out of the hands of purely religious teachers, and welded into a system that could be run by the State and could include modern subjects.

The government was then faced with an enormous task, which it has not yet finished. Such teachers as there were in Tunisia at the time of independence were mostly French. Before the Tunisians could train their own teachers, however, they had to educate them from the primary level upwards. Some secondary school pupils have been trained as teachers and have begun to teach after leaving school at nineteen. Expanding secondary and higher education is bound to take longer.

Tunisian children lining up to go into school

Many Tunisian parents had, and have, to be persuaded that education is necessary for their children. In the poorer, more traditional, agricultural areas education still does not always seem important; children can be useful at home, looking after flocks of sheep or helping on the land.

Tunisia has achieved more than many developing countries in the field of education—it is the largest single item in the budget every year. The numbers of children in school rise each year, but so do the overall numbers of children. Even primary education cannot yet be made compulsory, but it is free to all who can take it up.

Primary education is for children between the ages of six and twelve. It is conducted in Arabic, although French is taught from the third or fourth year. At the end of their sixth year in the primary school, children take an examination. About half of them pass this, and it forms the entrance examination to secondary education.

All those children who go on to secondary school take the same subjects for the first three years. After that, different groups specialize in areas such as technical education, training for specific jobs, teacher training, higher education in agriculture or entrance to university. In secondary school, subjects are taught in both Arabic and French, and English is taught as a foreign language.

There is a desperate need for more scientists and mathematicians, and higher education is expanding to meet this need. There is a new college called L'Ariana, near Tunis. It is highly selective, taking only the very best students, and it teaches all its scientific subjects in English. A new Faculty of Arts of the Tunisian University opened in Kairouan in 1985. And new teacher training centres are being set up all the time.

Of course, there are still inequalities in the system. The drop-out rate is very high at all levels. People who have been educated stand out obviously from those who have not, simply because of their ability to speak French. More boys than girls are educated, although ten times as many girls were educated in 1984 as in 1956, which shows a real change. Far more children go to school in the large towns and villages of the coastal areas than in the small towns and settlements of the poorer interior.

Yet the message seems to be getting through. It is very touching to see groups of tiny children, immaculately dressed in colourful overalls and with satchels on their backs, trudging sturdily to classes across a wide, dusty landscape in which, as far as the eye can see, there is no obvious sign of home or school.

Every year, when school starts again after the summer holidays, the newspapers make it one of their main stories, giving details of the numbers of children going to school and reporting interviews with children who say why they are glad to be going back. Everything is being done to encourage parents to send their children to school, particularly by educating mothers.

In many Islamic countries, women scarcely ever appear out of doors in the towns and the few who do are heavily veiled. This is no longer true in Tunisia where women jostle their way through the rush-hour crowds along with men. In Tunis, women police help to control the traffic.

Many women, even young ones, wear the traditional light white veil, the *safsari*. They drape this over the head (leaving the face free) and then round the body to just above the ankles. Some older women hold it drawn over the lower part of the face. The reasons for wearing the veil are often entirely practical. The *safsari* is particularly popular during the winter, and when dusty winds are blowing in the summer. Younger women will occasionally fling it on when they want to go out without bothering to change their clothes or to make up their faces.

This does not mean that all Tunisian women yet have, or even want, the kind of freedom that European or American women take for granted. Many Tunisian married women spend their days in their husband's courtyard, almost entirely in the company of other women, not even going out to shop. It is deeply-rooted religious and cultural attitudes, together with economic difficulties, that prevent their freedom—not government policy.

Some Tunisian men complain that President Bourguiba is too kind to women. There is no doubt that he had their interests at heart when he introduced the Personal Liberties Code (one of his first reforms) in 1956. This attempted to redefine marriage, making it a relationship between two equal people, rather than a contract by which a man came to own a woman as he might own any other goods.

First, the Code said that a man could no longer have more

A street scene in Tunis showing men and women wearing traditional and modern clothing

Wedding festivities in the south of Tunisia

than one wife at a time; polygamy was now illegal. Perhaps even more importantly, it said that a woman had to agree to being married of her own free will; she could no longer be forced into marriage. In addition, the minimum age of seventeen was set for marriage so that very young girls could no longer be sold off as brides by their families. Husbands could no longer divorce their wives simply by saying they wanted to, which is what they had done in the past. For the first time, women as well as men could start divorce proceedings.

Some of these ideas are taking a long time to be accepted in remote areas. Seventeen is now the most popular age for girls to marry—that is, at the earliest possible age. Yet the Code has made a great difference to Tunisian women in general, and probably gives them the possibility of more dignity and equality than any other Islamic women. Greater change cannot come without increased education and prosperity.

In 1957 Bourguiba himself encouraged the formation of a Woman's Union, the *Union Nationale des Femmes de Tunisie* (UNFT). This was an attempt to educate women politically, because in that year they were given the vote for the first time in Tunisian history. Since mothers are the main educators of very young children, it seemed vital to free women from their very restricted lives so that they could broaden their children's horizons. The Union still plays an active part in politics.

In 1983, two women were appointed to the Cabinet for the first time—one as Minister for Family Affairs and the Advancement of Women, and one as Minister of State for Public Health. These posts illustrate the importance given to health education for women. They are taught how to prevent the diseases that arise from insanitary conditions, and they are also taught how to limit their families. Because Tunisians marry young and are now better cared for, they produce many healthy children. The government would like to control the growth of population, and it was one of the first in Africa to set up a family planning programme.

Family planning centres are only one element in a whole set of basic health structures scattered throughout the country. These include mother and child centres and rural and communal dispensaries. The prevention of illness has a high priority, and

Tunisia has almost wiped out diseases such as tuberculosis, trachoma, typhus, polio and diphtheria that are often found in Third World countries. More hospitals are being built all the time, and bringing better health care to remote areas. Many French doctors left the country at the time of independence, but these have now been replaced, and there is a constant attempt to increase the number of doctors. Even small towns now have clinics, where treatment is good, and free for those who cannot afford to pay.

Tunisian women have the possibility of a better life than most women in developing countries. However, a young woman teacher or bank clerk in Tunis is still worlds apart from the wife of a poor farmer in the interior. They seem almost to live in different periods of history. One may be educated, fashionably dressed, living a comparatively independent life; the other may be illiterate, tied to work in her home and her husband's fields, waiting on her menfolk, and interminably bound by the need to fetch all the water she uses in the home.

Even in the mountainous region of the north-west, where there is plenty of rain, women of all ages can be seen making their way, barefooted and easily, down steep and crumbling paths with a heavy container of water in either hand, or with a water pot strapped to their heads. Their young daughters follow with bright little plastic containers of their own, learning their role for the future. Social life for these women centres round the moments of easy gossip while they pause to wash themselves and fill their water pots at the nearest well or spring.

Agriculture and Fishing

Agriculture is the most important feature of the Tunisian economy. Almost half the population earn their living by it, and it must still be expanded in order to feed the country's growing population and to increase food exports.

Four problems have proved difficult to overcome: the ownership and organization of land, the very erratic water supply, soil erosion, and the arid climate of the south. No government can do much about the climate, but attempts are being made to deal with the other problems.

After independence, the new Tunisian government gradually took back land that had been held by the French colonists until, in 1964, all agricultural land still owned by foreigners was nationalized. In those early years, the new government attempted to collectivize land, urging farmers to work co-operatively, to share their lands and profits. A combination of dry years, poor harvests and resistance to this policy by farmers persuaded the government to abandon the policy in 1969. Since then, land has been owned in a mixture of ways, so that now about sixty per cent is owned privately, twenty per cent co-operatively and twenty per cent by the state.

The supply of water to the land is probably the central problem of Tunisian agriculture. The agricultural areas have

The Beni M'tir dam south of Ain Draham. Tunisia is undertaking a huge water-development programme with a view to conserving water and preventing disastrous flooding of productive land

rain in the winter, but ninety per cent of it evaporates, is immediately absorbed by the soil or actually causes floods. This means that less than ten per cent reaches and remains in the rivers. Tunisia is undertaking a huge water development programme, building dams both to conserve this water and to prevent disastrous flooding of productive land. In many cases tree planting has to go along with dam construction, or water simply takes the top soil with it into the new reservoirs and silts them up.

Top soil has been eroded in many parts of the country over the years. Goats have been allowed to graze too much in some places; in other places land that is really unsuitable for growing crops has been shallow-ploughed for many years by people desperate to produce food for themselves. These problems were made worse during the French Protectorate when small farmers were driven from the best lands by colonizers. In some areas it is still possible to see terracing on poor, dry hillsides that look unfit even for growing vines, where wheat was actually grown by Tunisians who had been driven off the better land in the valley during French rule.

If Tunisia can overcome these problems, the prospects for agriculture are good. The country is already making good progress towards growing a greater variety of crops, increasing the use of fertilizers and making more use of machinery. Systems of farming vary according to the region and the resources available. Extreme contrasts can still be seen just a short distance from each other—one man uses a camel to drag a wooden plough that has scarcely changed in form since Roman times, another man ploughs with the aid of the most up-to-date tractor available. In some places irrigation schemes provide sophisticated drip systems for market gardens; in others people must carry every drop of water to plants and animals.

Wherever conditions make it possible, the government is encouraging people to settle in houses in villages rather than to continue their nomadic or semi-nomadic existence. Houses may be less picturesque than the tents of the nomads but they

A camel-drawn plough near El Jem

probably give a good deal more protection from the weather. It is interesting to see how rapidly new villages are springing up by the roadside in most of the fertile areas. Houses are simply constructed, to a traditional pattern, and people seem to be able to build their own and to help one another.

The fishing industry has not yet developed sufficiently well to please the Tunisians. This is partly because of shortage of money to replace worn-out equipment and to construct boats suitable for long-range fishing trips. Demand for fish is growing and it means that more money will have to be invested in equipment for boats and in fishing ports, to provide cold storage and warehouses, for example.

Opportunities for growth exist, as Tunisia is particularly rich in fish. There is a wide shelf of rock in fairly shallow water off

Traditional boats in the fishing port of Gabès. Although Tunisia's fishing industry is not yet highly developed, demand for fish is growing and there are promising opportunities for future growth

the east coast. This harbours plankton and vegetation that attracts shoals of fish. If you order fish in a Tunisian restaurant the cook will often show you a great earthenware dish holding an example of each kind of fish he has, from which to choose. These raw fish, artistically arranged on a platter, look just like the precisely-drawn fish on Roman mosaics made sixteen centuries ago.

As well as sea fish, there is a promising programme for aquaculture—the cultivation of certain kinds of freshwater fish, particularly shellfish. It seems likely that lakes and reservoirs that have been created for irrigation are going to be used for this programme.

Industry, Tourism and Crafts

When Tunisia became independent in 1956 it had little industry worth the name. It even had to import ninety-five per cent of the raw materials needed to provide energy. Although there were some small-scale, scattered manufacturing industries serving local communities, the few sizeable industries were concentrated near the coast, near the ports that would export their products to France. Tunisia's minerals and agricultural products were exported in their raw form, as they usually are from undeveloped or colonized countries. In this form they have comparatively little value. It is the country that processes and markets the products that makes money from them.

In 1956 the Tunisians needed jobs throughout the country, not just near the coast. They needed to manufacture their own goods, and so save money on imports. They also needed foreign money with which to buy essential goods from other countries. To get this money they had to make goods to export. They needed to develop a regular supply of energy. They needed to train people to manufacture the goods, and to sell them abroad.

In an attempt to grapple with these needs, national economic plans have set out successive tasks and have so far been more effective in shaping industry than agriculture. Since 1961, the government can claim a constant increase in investment and growth in industrial production.

The country no longer has to import its energy. In fact, at the moment its main export is petroleum. Since the first discovery of oil at El Borma in southern Tunisia, near the Algerian border, other oil fields have been found off the coasts. Nevertheless there is probably a limited amount of oil there, and the country expects to have less than enough for its own needs by some time in the 1990s.

Tunisia's production of electricity for public use has risen steadily, with eighteen power stations already built, and more planned. A nuclear reactor is planned at Gabès, and electricity will be an increasingly used source of energy.

As well as oil, Tunisia has minerals such as iron ore, lead and zinc, but it is richest in phosphates. Phosphates, and the fertilizers made from them, form the country's second most important export. In fact, Tunisia is the third most important exporter of phosphoric acid in the world. It no longer simply exports cheap crude phosphates as it did under the French Protectorate, but has developed a heavy chemical industry based on processing phosphates, so adding value to the product and creating more jobs. Processing plants have been set up in Gabès and Gafsa, towns in the south—a part of the country often neglected in the past.

In a similar way, the government has invested in the food industry—in flour-milling, sugar-refining, poultry farming and processing, butter- and yoghurt-making, tomato-canning, tobacco production, mineral-water bottling, and so on. All these activities provide jobs in agricultural areas, and also add value to the original products.

The emphasis in the sixth plan (1982-1986) was on the mechanical and electrical industries which manufacture the goods Tunisia needs so badly. These industries, and the metallurgical industry, are expanding steadily and have attracted some foreign investment. By agreement with the other countries involved, Tunisia is now assembling German, French and American cars and is expanding its manufacture of much-needed farm machinery. The emphasis in the next national economic plan is on the electric and electronic industries, which are relatively new to Tunisia.

An olive-press worker at Matmata. Olive oil is one of Tunisia's most important exports

Another modern industry is the production of cement, which is increasing every year. One of its main uses must be in the construction of the hotels and swimming-pools which are the obvious sign of Tunisia's fastest-growing industry—tourism.

Tourism was the nation's largest foreign currency earner from 1968-1976, but was then overtaken by petroleum. Its importance to the country was shown by the creation in 1983 of a Ministry of Tourism and Handicrafts. Tourism is a vital sector of the economy because it employs so many people, directly and indirectly.

There are now five schools of tourism and a Higher Institute of Tourism and Hotel Management in Tunisia. Students attend these in the winter months and work in the industry during the summer. Such schools are guaranteeing a high standard of service in Tunisian hotels.

Visitors to Tunisia can choose to eat the "continental" type of food offered in hotels throughout Europe, or food that has been influenced by French cuisine, or the kind of food Tunisians themselves eat. Of course, food eaten in Tunisian homes is rather different from that served in hotels and restaurants, but these do offer many characteristic dishes.

For most people the staple meal is *couscous*. This is based on semolina, which is steamed above a stew or soup of vegetables, meat or chicken so that it absorbs all the flavours. The juices and pieces of meat and vegetables, all deliciously spiced, are then served on a bed of the semolina. This is the North African equivalent of the rice, pasta or potatoes eaten elsewhere.

Turkish rule influenced Tunisian cooking, so that kebabs of lamb or fish are common; so are sweet pastries, stuffed with nuts and dates and soaked in honey. Tunisians love hot chilli peppers and Europeans often ask for their food to be less "piquant" to avoid the strongest effect of these. A sauce called *harissa*—made of minced red peppers, salt, and garlic softened in oil—is usually on the table and can be added even to soup. A favourite salad is *mechouia*, which is a mixture of green peppers, tomatoes, chillies, onions and garlic, which have been grilled to sweeten them and to make the skins easy to remove. Once peeled, they are minced and spiced and sometimes decorated with capers, tuna and slices of egg. *Shorba*, or soup, whether made of meat or fish, is usually a meal in itself in Tunisia. Various kinds of roasts and slow-cooked stews are prepared with herbs and spices.

A good fast food is an egg *brik*, which is a triangle of paper-thin pastry containing an egg together with chopped parsley and capers. The whole thing is deep fried so that inside the crisp pastry the egg white is cooked and the yolk is still just soft. *Briks* are often served as a first course in restaurants, but they can also be bought at roadside stalls, where the secret of making them is revealed. They are always eaten with the fingers, and often leave egg on the face.

Perhaps the greatest treat for the foreigner in Tunisia is the local fish and fruit. There is a great variety and abundance of Mediterranean fish and shellfish. These are all cooked simply and deliciously. Fruit is always fresh and varies according to the season—perfect melons, grapes, peaches, figs, dates, pomegranates and oranges, for example. Another delight is the sweet mint tea, served in glasses, that is so refreshing after a day in the Tunisian sun.

Although Tunisia is a Muslim country, the French have left a tradition of vine-growing and Tunisian wines are probably the best in North Africa.

The country is now anxious to diversify its tourist attractions. Visitors came at first to bask in the sun on Tunisian's wide, sandy beaches. Now they are offered more than sea and sunshine. The first of a number of planned tourist complexes has been completed, at Port el Kantaoui, near Sousse. It has a harbour and marina, many sports and recreation facilities and shopping areas. It is a modern version of a typical Tunisian harbour town, but with everything planned for ease and leisure rather than for work.

It is only one of many bases for sailing-boats, and there are unlimited opportunities for other water sports, such as underwater fishing and water skiing, in Tunisia's warm sea. The most spectacular fishing event is the annual catch of tunny fish in the spring and early summer at Sidi Daoud. This is the *matanza*, where the huge fish swim into a net that gradually narrows into a trap. When the trap is full of fish and has been hauled into the shallows, men jump into the water and kill the fish with knives and gaffs. More peaceful and conventional fishing trips can also be arranged with local fishermen.

It is possible to ride horses or camels on the beaches and in

The beach in Hammamet, one of Tunisia's most popular resorts

the countryside. Horseriding is particularly popular in the northern mountains, where there is also game-shooting and organized boar-hunting. Further south, near a village called El Haouaria, falcons are trapped in the spring and trained in time to catch the quail as they migrate across the tip of Tunisia at Cap Bon. Many people go to El Haouaria for the falconry festival which is held there in June.

Tourist complexes are planned at Tabarka, on the north coast, and at Ain Draham, a town in the hills of the north-west that is reminiscent of an Alpine village. The Ministry of Tourism also wants to encourage more tourists to visit the country in the winter. The sun of the Sahara has much to offer European visitors in December and January.

Tourists enjoying a camel ride in the oasis town of Douz

In every case, strenuous efforts are being made to protect the way of life and traditions of the inhabitants of the area concerned, although it is obviously impossible for them not to be affected by tourists. Care is also being taken to protect the landscape. In Hammamet, for example, no hotel is allowed to rise above the tops of the trees. In this way dozens of hotels are hidden away in fragrant, shady gardens and they have not been allowed to destroy the peaceful beauty their visitors came to enjoy. At the moment, in developing Saharan tourism, the Ministry is at pains to preserve the unique beauty of the area and the thrill of isolation and danger which it gives to tourists while actually allowing them to have a safe and comfortable holiday.

The development of tourism in Tunisia has not affected

traditional Islamic festivals, such as Ramadan, but in many cases it has altered the popular non-religious festivals. Some of these, which were once celebrations of the harvest—such as the Palm Tree Festival in Tozeur—have opened out to include visitors and have become more general occasions for people to meet each other for public demonstrations of local folk-dancing and singing. Camel races have also proved popular with tourists and have sometimes developed into major festivities. By contrast there are the private wedding celebrations; these continue over at least three days, with a great deal of music. *Malouf* music seems the most characteristic sound of Tunisia; it is highly rhythmic and played on violins, lutes and drums.

As well as the country festivals, which occur throughout the summer, there are comparatively new international festivals that

Traditional musicians entertaining tourists at Nefta

Tozeur international airport

have been deliberately planned in certain locations. The festival at Dougga, for example, uses the impressive Roman theatre set on a hillside. Hammamet has a long international summer festival in its open-air theatre near the sea. Musicians, painters and singers mingle with holiday-makers at Tabarka for an open festival that runs right through June and July. It is safe to say that there is something interesting going on in most towns in Tunisia at some time in the summer.

Tourism in Tunisia is made easier by the communication system, which is of a high standard. One good legacy left by the French is a very useful network of railways, which has been extended recently: there are now more than 2,000 kilometres (1,250 miles) of track. There are five international airports: at Tunis, Monastir, Jerba, Tozeur and Sfax. Tunis takes two-thirds of the whole traffic. There are five ports: Tunis, Sfax, Bizerta, Gabès and Sousse. Tunis is the main port for passengers and also the main port for goods in terms of value. Sfax is the main port for goods in terms of tonnage, however. Bizerta transports mainly oil products, and Gabès is an oil terminal. Sousse is a smaller and more picturesque port, mainly used for the shipment of goods. The road links between all these facilities are good.

Tunisia has a tradition of fine craftsmanship, which it has been able to continue in the manufacture of textiles, leather goods—particularly shoes—ceramics, glass and furniture.

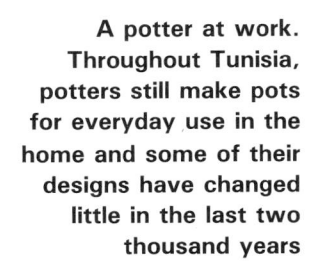

A potter at work. Throughout Tunisia, potters still make pots for everyday use in the home and some of their designs have changed little in the last two thousand years

Traditional Tunisian jewellery, showing the typical hand and fish motifs

Women in rural areas still make moulded pots; they spin and dye wool for the blankets they weave, make rugs and carpets, weave grass mats and embroider their wedding clothes.

Since Tunisia became independent, the government has taken an interest in small-scale handicrafts and has set up a Tunisian Handicrafts Board (ONAT). This encourages traditional regional specialization, and it has also helped to bring back to life some handicrafts that had almost died out, such as painting on glass. When they have completed their schooling, children with skills in particular crafts can develop them at special centres, and then they are often helped to set up their own workshops in their chosen crafts. For this reason handicrafts flourish in Tunisia, and those that carry the ONAT stamp are of a reliably high standard.

The people of certain areas continue to specialize or excel in particular crafts. For example, the pottery and decorated ceramic tiles made in in Nabeul are justly famous. From Gafsa come beautifully coloured blankets. Jerba's dyed wools are made into woollen rugs and shawls. Delicate and intricate white wire birdcages are made in Sidi Bou Said. Beautiful objects are created from olivewood, leather, beaten copper and wrought iron in a number of areas, and simple everyday pots and storage jars are made throughout the country. Jewellery is traditionally both an investment and a way of displaying wealth. Silver jewellery is particularly fine in Tunisia. The most sought-after hand-made goods are probably the carpets of Kairouan. The women who make these visit the mosques and shrines of their holy city to copy patterns from the ancient tiles on the walls and floors there.

The motifs used by women in carpet-making, embroidery and weaving are interesting in themselves. The religion of Islam forbids the representation of the human form in art. Women, especially in the Sahara, sometimes weave human figures into their rugs, but it is chiefly trees, flowers, birds and animals that are used to decorate Tunisian textiles, leather, ceramics, wood and jewellery. Two favourite motifs are the *Khomsa* and the fish. The *Khomsa* is an open hand, sometimes called the hand of

A popular woven design from the Sahel area, part of Tunisia's long tradition which still persists in the twentieth century

Fatima, and its origins are ancient and mysterious. Both the hand and the fish are regarded as kindly, protective, good-luck signs in Tunisia, and are so familiar that they are sometimes represented merely by a kind of geometrical outline.

The Future

Tunisia probably has an interesting but difficult time ahead. It has the advantage of a well-established political system. Unless the country can attract more foreign investment, however, there will be a limit to its industrial development. The oil is not likely to last for ever, and this will mean loss of income for the state.

If Tunisia can keep its population from growing too large, it could provide the people with reasonable living conditions. Improvements in agriculture should produce good results, although the climate will always set some limits. Many Tunisians see tourism as one of their most important ways of earning money and creating a good future. They would certainly approve of the idea *"Let's visit Tunisia"*.

Index

Abbasids 45
agriculture *see* crops and cultivation
Africa 7, 11, 13, 30, 35
Africa Proconsularis 35
Aghlabids 45-47
Ahmed Bey 53
Ain Draham 85
airports 88
Algeria 11, 13, 17, 24, 30, 50, 51, 54
alphabet 33
animals 20, 25, 26, 30, 76, 84-85, 87, 91
Arabic language 9, 10, 49, 58, 68
Arabs 8, 41-49
L'Ariana College 68
Asia 30
Atlas Mountains 13-16, 19

Baghdad 45
Banu Hilal 48
Banu Sulaym 48
Bedouin 7, 48
Béja 18
Berbers 8, 31, 33, 40, 43, 44, 47, 49, 50
Bizerta 10, 14, 18, 89
Bizerta, Lake of 17
boundaries 30, 35, 50, 52
Bourguiba, President Habib 59, 60, 61, 62-65, 72
bread riots 65
Bulla Regia 37
Byzantine, Byzantium 40, 42, 43, 51

Cap Bon 14, 19
Carthage 32-35, 40, 43
children 11-12, 67-69, 72
chotts 24-25
Christianity, Christians 39, 44, 49, 50, 52

climate 14, 19-23, 28, 30, 74, 93
clothes 7, 69, 73
collectivization of land 74
communications 88-89
Constantine, Emperor 39
Constantinople 51
constitution 59, 62, 65
crafts and craftsmen 23, 29, 57, 89-92
crops and cultivation 17-22, 25, 33, 35-36, 38, 52, 56, 76

Damascus 45
Destour Party *see also* Néo Destour Party *and* Socialist Destour Party 59
Dorsale see High Tell
Dougga 37, 88
Douz 25
dry farming 22

economic plans 79-81
education 57-58, 66-69
Egypt 42, 47
El Borma 24, 26, 80
electricity 80
El Hamma 25
El Haouaria 85
Elissa, Queen of Carthage 32
El Jem 37, 39
El Kef (Le Kef) 18
employment 12, 57, 74, 79-82, 90
English language 68
European Economic Community 11
exports 52, 80

farming *see* crops and cultivation
Fatimah 45
Fatimids 47-48
festivals 86-88
fishing 26, 77-78, 84
food 82-84

94

France and the French 8, 9, 11, 53-54, 55-61, 64, 66, 73, 74, 76, 79, 80, 81, 82, 84
French language 10, 68

Gabès 24, 26, 27, 80, 89
Gafsa 24, 80, 91
ghorfas 27-28
Great Eastern Erg 24, 25
Greeks (ancient) 31
Grombalia, plain of 19

Hadrumetum 32
Hafsids 49-50
Hammamet 19, 86, 88
Hammamet, Gulf of 22
health care 72-73
High Tell *(Dobale)* 14, 16, 17, 19
Husainids 52-54

Ibn Khaldun 48
Ifriqiyah 43, 49
independence (from France) 9, 59, 60, 62, 65, 66, 74, 79, 90
industry 18, 26, 57, 79-82, 93
irrigation 17, 33, 35, 74-75, 76
Islam, Islamic belief and culture 9, 11, 21, 41-42, 44-47, 49-51, 56, 58, 60, 64, 65, 66, 72, 87
Istanbul 40, 51
Italians 8, 57, 60

Jerba, island of 28, 49, 91
Jews 8

Kahina 44
Kairouan 21, 22, 43, 44, 45-46, 50, 91
Kasserine 20
Kebili 25
Kroumir Mountains 15-17, 54
Kuwait 12

land ownership 56-57, 74, 76
landscape 7, 13-29, 86
language 9
Lebanon 31
Le Kef *see* El Kef
Libya 11, 12, 24, 30, 35, 52
Libyic people 31
limes 35

Maghreb 13, 30, 31, 42
Mahdia 47
Maktar 37
malouf music 87
Maltese 8
marriage 70-72
Matmata 27
Mecca 41, 47
Medenine 27
Medina 42
medina 9
Mediterranean Sea and region 7, 13, 30-32, 40, 45, 49-51, 83-84
Menzel Bourguiba 18
Middle East 11
minerals 26, 80
Monastir 22
Morocco 11, 13
Muhammad 41, 42, 44-45
Muslim *see* Islam
Mzali, Prime Minister 64

Nabeul 19, 91
Nefta 25
Néo-Destour party 59, 61-63
nomads 7, 20, 24, 30, 31, 35, 39, 49, 56, 57, 76
Normans 49
Numidia 35, 43

oases 25-26
oil (petroleum) 24, 26, 80, 93
ONAT (Tunisian Handicrafts Board) 90-91

95

Ottoman Empire *see* Turks
oued 19

Personal Liberties Code 70
Phoenicians 8, 31
population 7, 8, 12, 18-19, 30, 31, 57, 72, 93
Port el Kantaoui 84
ports 89
prehistoric period 30
privateers 50, 52
Protectorate *see* France
Punic wars 33

Qayrawan 43
Quran 9

railways 88
rainfall 14, 16, 22, 23
Ramadan 87
religion *see* Islam
ribats 46-47
Romans (ancient) 8, 28, 33-39, 76, 78

Sadiki College 58, 59
safsari 7, 69
Sahara Desert 7, 13, 14, 23-25, 30, 35, 43, 85, 86, 91
Sahel 14, 19-22
Saudi Arabia 12, 41, 42
Second World War 60
settlement policy 76-77
Sfax 9, 19, 22, 33, 46, 89
Shi'ite Muslims 45, 47
Sicily 13, 19, 33, 49
Sidi Bou Said 91
Sidi Daoud 84
Sidon 32
Socialist Destour Party 63
soil erosion 21, 74, 76
souks 9
Sousse 9, 22, 32, 46, 84, 89

Spain 42, 44
Spanish Muslims (Andalusians) 50
sport 84-85
steppe land 14, 19, 20-22, 43
Sufetula 37
Sunni Muslims 45

Tabarka 85, 88
Tatouine 27
Tell *see also* High Tell 15
terracing 33, 76
Thuburbo Majus 37
tourism 28, 29, 82, 84-89, 93
Tozeur 25, 87
Tripolitania 35, 42, 50, 51
Tunis 9, 12, 14, 19, 44, 46, 50, 52, 57, 59, 60, 73, 88-89
Tunis, Gulf of 17, 19, 30, 31, 32, 44
Turks, Turkish influence 8, 50-53, 83
Tyre 32

UGGT (Union of Tunisian Workers) 60, 64
UNFT (Union of Tunisian Women) 72
United Nations Organization 60
University of Tunis 66
Uqba ibn Nafi 43
Utica 32

Vandals 40

wadi *see oued*
water supply *see also* irrigation *and* rainfall 21-22, 24, 25, 46, 73, 74-75, 76
women 7, 69-73, 91

Zenata tribes 43
Ziri, Zirids 47-48
Zitouna Mosque and University 46, 58, 66